BUFFALO BILL HISTORICAL CENTER • CODY, WYOMING

Treasures
From Our West

TABLE OF CONTENTS

FOLLOWING PAGE:
*THE ROUGH RIDERS OF THE WORLD IN
A GRAND ETHNOLOGICAL CONGRESS*
(DETAIL).

PREVIOUS PAGE:
ALBERT BIERSTADT.
YELLOWSTONE FALLS (DETAIL).

The vast American West was once utterly uncharted. Its unmatched beauty and broad horizons were home to Native American peoples for hundreds of years before beckoning and beguiling settlers and pioneers from the East. These two cultures, sometimes in harmony, sometimes in conflict, made an indelible mark upon the land and its history.

Much of that pioneering spirit was embodied in a man, William Frederick Cody, whose name and dynamism are at the core of this institution. Cody,

revered as Buffalo Bill, brought the essence of the American West to the world. Through him and his renowned Wild West show the nation shared the allure and inspiration of the West.

Cody died in 1917, but he, and the West in which he lived, did not vanish. At his passing the Buffalo Bill Memorial Association was chartered. A nonprofit educational organization, its purpose is to preserve the story, philosophy, and art of our western heritage—the heritage once so vividly represented to the world by Buffalo Bill.

HERMON ATKINS MACNEIL (1866–1947).
THE SUN VOW, MODELED 1899, CAST 1919.
BRONZE; CAST BY ROMAN BRONZE WORKS; HEIGHT 34¼ IN.
As a young artist, MacNeil developed an interest in Indian subjects when he saw Buffalo Bill's Wild West show perform during the World's Columbian Exposition in Chicago. Inspired by the dignity and grace of the Indians he saw there, he sought to create sculptures following ideals from ancient and Renaissance art.
Gift of William F. Davidson and John J. Cunningham, by exchange.

BUFFALO BILL, C. 1913.
By the turn of the century Buffalo Bill had become one of the most famous men in the world, a hero and role model for millions of children. He doted on his five grandchildren and his many nieces and nephews.

In 1927, in keeping with its stated goals, the Association opened its original museum, an elegant log building patterned after Cody's TE Ranch house. Under the aegis of the Association, and with the help of its friends and benefactors, the concept of the original museum has grown and flourished to become the four museums and the library of the Buffalo Bill Historical Center.

The Buffalo Bill Museum presents the memorabilia and mementos of Buffalo Bill and his West; the Whitney Gallery of Western Art features an unsurpassed collection of western art; the Plains Indian Museum explores the culture of Native American people of the western plains; and the Cody Firearms Museum traces the development of projectile weapons. Each museum exemplifies the West; together they trace patterns of life that are uniquely American.

The Buffalo Bill Historical Center offers visitors provocative insights into the historic American West. The art and artifacts they find represent the mythic as well as factual past. This is a story of great accomplishment, profound tragedy, and bright promise. Here is evidence of how the Native American and EuroAmerican cultures clashed and intertwined in a compelling human drama. Here are signs of how the West contributed to our nation's complex cultural fabric. And here also is clear proof of how this vast, rugged region influenced evolving American artistic traditions. All are part of this unique museum encounter with the West.

MOCCASINS, MESQUAKIE, C. 1880.
LENGTH 10¼ IN.; HEIGHT 2⅞ IN.; WIDTH 4⅞ IN.
Innovative design and use of color by the Eastern Plains and Prairie people are shown in the checkerboard and floral beadwork of these moccasins.
Chandler-Pohrt Collection,
Gift of the Pilot Foundation.

ALFRED JACOB MILLER (1810–1874).
THE LOST GREENHORN, C. 1866.
OIL ON CANVAS; 17⅛ x 23⅞ IN.
Miller accompanied a caravan taking supplies to the fur traders' rendezvous in 1837. In this painting the artist portrayed the caravan's cook who became lost on the great prairie when he set out alone to go buffalo hunting. Miller's image also seems to symbolize the romanticism of westward expansion, with the independent figure looking resolutely into the distance.
Gift of The Coe Foundation.

AMERICAN AIR PISTOL,
C. 1871–1872. .25 CALIBER.
OVERALL LENGTH 10¼ IN.;
BARREL LENGTH 5¼ IN.
Widely marketed after the Civil War, low-cost air pistols such as this one by E. H. Hawley were intended for indoor use. Target shooting with air pistols was a popular and inexpensive form of entertainment.

BUFFALO BILL'S BOYHOOD HOME.
BUILT IN LECLAIRE, IOWA, 1841.
The Cody family lived in this house for two years before
moving to Kansas in 1854. The house was purchased by
the Chicago, Burlington and Quincy Railroad, moved to
Cody in 1933, and given to the Buffalo Bill Memorial
Association in 1948.

PENDANT LOCKET, 1892.
Gold and diamonds encircle the monogram for "Victoria
Regina." The back is of garnet and bloodstone pressed
together and inscribed, "Her Majesty, Queen Victoria to
Col. W. F. Cody June 25 1892."

GERTRUDE VANDERBILT WHITNEY (1877–1942).
BUFFALO BILL—THE SCOUT, 1922–1924.
BRONZE; CAST BY ROMAN BRONZE WORKS;
HEIGHT 12 FT. 5 IN.

In 1922 Gertrude Vanderbilt Whitney was commissioned to create a monumental bronze sculpture of William F. "Buffalo Bill" Cody. In this dynamic equestrian sculpture, she depicted Cody in his historic role as a scout, bending down to read the trail while signaling with his rifle.

Gift of the artist.

Within just three generations after the Civil War, the entire trans-Mississippi West was crisscrossed with railroads and filled in with states. Settlement was rapid and disorderly. Americans felt that they were "winning" the West, and that it was America's destiny to tame and reclaim the wilderness and make the land economically productive.

If the experience seemed epic, no one better defined it for Americans and Europeans than Buffalo Bill Cody. And nothing turned the epic into an orderly narrative better than Buffalo Bill's Wild West show.

William Frederick Cody was born in 1846 in a log cabin two miles west of the Mississippi River in Iowa Territory. His father took the family to Kansas in 1854 where young Will became part of—or witness to—the events that shaped the West. He joined a gold rush, became an expert horseman and marksman, trapped beaver, drove a stagecoach, and worked for the Pony Express.

During the Civil War Cody fought for the Union with the 7th Kansas Cavalry. In 1866 he married a St. Louis girl, Louisa Frederici, who did not entirely succeed in domesticating him during their fifty-one-year marriage.

He earned his greatest fame as a hunter, guide, and scout for the army during the Indian wars. Then he was persuaded to go on stage, portraying himself in "border dramas," and he spent the rest of his life in show business.

Buffalo Bill started his Wild West show in Nebraska in 1883 and spent thirty years on the road, ten of them in Europe. He sank the profits from his shows into projects to help develop the modern West. Though most of them did not pay off, the legacy of his investments can be found in Arizona, Nebraska, and especially in his namesake city, Cody, Wyoming. He died in Denver in 1917 and was buried on top of Lookout Mountain overlooking the Colorado plains.

The Buffalo Bill Museum is home to many of the personal collections of W. F. Cody and his family, as well as to a vast array of objects related to his associates, his careers, and his Wild West show. The exhibition serves two purposes: to examine the personal and public lives of Buffalo Bill, and to interpret his story in the context of the history and myth of the American West.

ABOVE:
MEDAL OF HONOR.
Presented by "The Congress to William F. Cody, Guide, for GALLANTRY, at Platte River, Nebr., April 26, 1872." Only four Medals of Honor were awarded to civilian scouts and guides during the Indian wars. Though these medals were rescinded in 1916 because the recipients were civilians, full honors were restored by the Army in 1989.

PAWNEE AND SIOUX INDIANS, 1886.
Left to right: (Pawnee) Brave Chief, Eagle Chief, Knife Chief, Young Chief; Buffalo Bill; (Sioux) American Horse, Rocky Bear, Flies Above, Long Wolf. Photograph by Anderson, New York. The Pawnee and Sioux were traditional enemies on the Plains but found common ground in the wild West.

RIGHT:
IRVING R. BACON (1875–1962).
THE LIFE I LOVE (DETAIL), 1902.
OIL ON CANVAS; 22 x 34 IN.
During the big game hunt commemorated in this painting, Col. William F. "Buffalo Bill" Cody chose the site for his hunting lodge, Pahaska Tepee, near the east entrance to Yellowstone National Park. Iron Tail and Black Fox, who had appeared in Cody's Wild West, and Bishop George Allen Beecher appear in the full painting.
Bequest in memory of the Houx and Newell Families.

FOUR DECADES OF GOVERNMENT ISSUE:
CIVIL-WAR ERA INFANTRYMAN'S AMMUNITION POUCH;
CAVALRY SERGEANT'S FATIGUE BLOUSE, 1874 AND CAMPAIGN HAT, 1875;
VOLUNTEER MILITIA OFFICER'S DRESS SHOULDER BOARDS, C. 1890.

In 1868 only 2,600 soldiers manned the trails, railroad routes, and garrisons of the Great Plains. During the frontier period, the army relied to an extraordinary extent on the loyalty, resourcefulness, and mobility of officers and men, and on the special skills and knowledge of civilian scouts and guides such as Buffalo Bill Cody.

BUFFALO-HIDE COAT, C. 1872.
REMINGTON RIFLE, C. 1873.
Many civilian scouts during the Indian wars assumed flamboyant nicknames and adopted styles inspired by the dress and adornment of the Indian people among whom they lived and fought. Buffalo Bill was no exception. His buffalo-hide coat was trimmed with beaver fur and decorated with beadwork and bright tradecloth. This highly embellished rifle was presented to Cody by the Remington Company at its New York state factory in 1873.
Rifle:
Gift of Mr. and Mrs. Harry Schloss.

W. F. CODY, C. 1869.
GREEN RIVER KNIFE, C. 1865.
This is the earliest photograph of W. F. Cody as a young scout. From a tintype, image reversed. He sits on the left with his Springfield rifle, "Lucretia Borgia." The other civilian and the two cavalry officers are unidentified. Many scouts adapted Plains Indian styles, as this Green River knife with its brass tack-decorated sheath illustrates.

Transportation in America has always suggested adventure. Travel on the frontier was a process of discovery. The means of transportation became symbols of romance —the steamboat, the clipper ship, and in the West, the stagecoach.

CONCORD COACH, 1867.
Buffalo Bill owned and used this stagecoach in his Wild West. It is so called because it was made by the Abbot-Downing Company of Concord, New Hampshire, painted at the factory, and shipped west. *Gift of Olive and Glenn E. Nielson.*

RIGHT:
CONCORD COACH
RUNNING GEAR (DETAIL).
The stagecoach carried people in relative comfort over the rough roads of early America. The passenger compartment floated on two sets of leather springs called thoroughbraces. The motion of the coach, as Mark Twain wrote, was not unlike the rocking of a small boat.

WINCHESTER RIFLE,
MODEL 1892. .32 CALIBER.
OVERALL LENGTH 40 IN.

Though she was never a shareholder, Annie Oakley, "Little Sure Shot," was one of the show's greatest assets between 1884 and 1901. This goldplated rifle was made for Annie Oakley in 1896.
Gift of Mr. and Mrs. Spencer T. Olin.

BUFFALO BILL'S WILD WEST STOCK CERTIFICATE No. 1, 1887.
Buffalo Bill's Wild West began as a partnership and was incorporated before going to England for the first time. Certificate number one was issued to Cody, and number two to his business partner, Nate Salsbury.
Gift of DeForest and Duer.

AMBER, BLUE, AND PURPLE
GLASS TARGET BALLS, C. 1890.
The amber glass target ball was in Annie
Oakley's collection.
*Amber glass: Arnott Millett Collection,
courtesy of Mr. and Mrs. William Self.
Blue and purple glass: Gift of Alex Kerr.*

It has been estimated that by 1900
over one billion words had been
published about Buffalo Bill, mostly
in dime novels like these. It is no
wonder that many people began to
doubt whether they could believe
anything that they read about him.

THE ROUGH RIDERS OF THE WORLD IN
A GRAND ETHNOLOGICAL CONGRESS
LITHOGRAPH POSTER, 1910.
This poster advertising Buffalo Bill's
Wild West, made by U.S. Litho
Russell-Morgan Print, Cincinnati.

BUFFALO BILL'S WILD WEST, 1890.
Hand-tinted photograph by Salviati
of Buffalo Bill and Indian members
of the Wild West in Venice.

BUFFALO BILL'S SADDLE, C. 1895.
MADE BY
COLLINS AND MORRISON OF OMAHA.
The saddle is shown with Buffalo
Bill's gear: a buffalo hide serape;
a braided leather bridle with six-
shooter bit made for him by a
prisoner in the Colorado State
Penitentiary; and beaded buckskin gauntlets.
*Gauntlets: Gift of Mrs. S. W. Harding
for the issue of James M. Allen, Sr.
and his wife, Alva Isham Allen.*

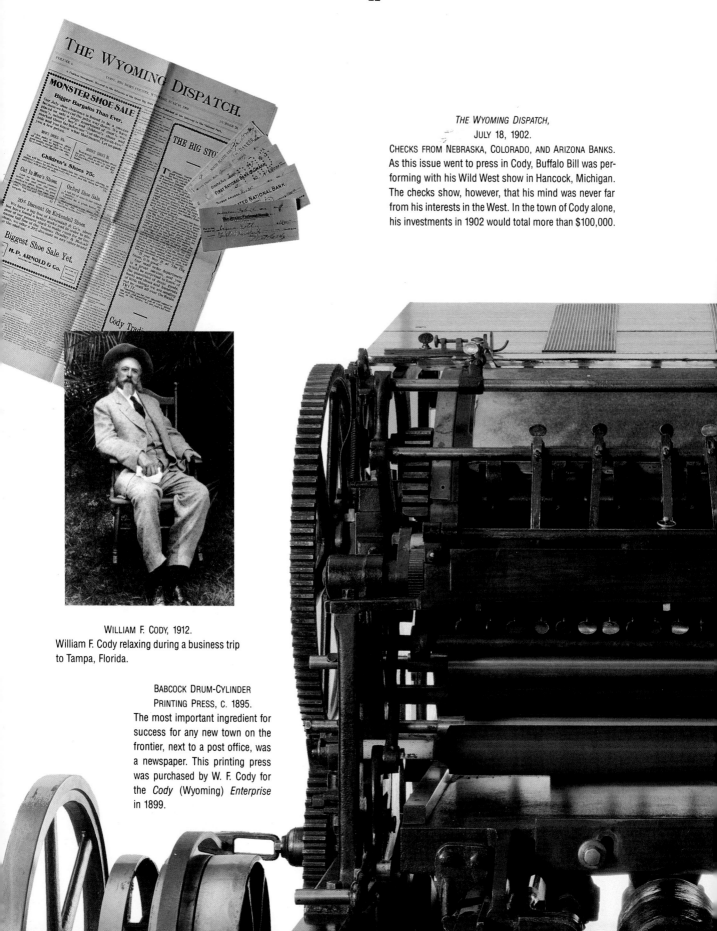

THE WYOMING DISPATCH,
JULY 18, 1902.
CHECKS FROM NEBRASKA, COLORADO, AND ARIZONA BANKS.
As this issue went to press in Cody, Buffalo Bill was performing with his Wild West show in Hancock, Michigan. The checks show, however, that his mind was never far from his interests in the West. In the town of Cody alone, his investments in 1902 would total more than $100,000.

WILLIAM F. CODY, 1912.
William F. Cody relaxing during a business trip to Tampa, Florida.

BABCOCK DRUM-CYLINDER
PRINTING PRESS, C. 1895.
The most important ingredient for success for any new town on the frontier, next to a post office, was a newspaper. This printing press was purchased by W. F. Cody for the *Cody* (Wyoming) *Enterprise* in 1899.

LETTER TO BUFFALO BILL FROM DAUGHTER ARTA, 1889.
ARTA CODY BOAL'S SILK MOIRE WEDDING DRESS, 1889.
W. F. Cody was in Europe with his Wild West when his daughter
Arta married Horton Boal at the family home in North Platte,
Nebraska; this is a letter she wrote on the eve of her wedding.
Only two of the Cody's four children survived to adulthood—
Arta, the eldest, and Irma Cody Garlow, the youngest.
*Dress: Gift of Mr. and Mrs. Robert Hayden
and Mr. Anthony Benn.*

EDISON CYLINDER PHONOGRAPH
AND CYLINDERS, C. 1900.
W. F. Cody and his family, like most
Americans, were excited by the
technological progress represented
by Thomas Edison's inventions.
Cody and Edison were equally celebrated by the French at the Centen-
nial Exposition in Paris in 1889, and
they became friends and mutual
admirers.

WHITNEY GALLERY OF WESTERN ART

The Whitney Gallery of Western Art presents the creative accomplishments of the artists who explored, documented, celebrated, and interpreted the American West. One of the most important collections of American western art, the Whitney gives a comprehensive overview of the development of western art from the early nineteenth century to the present day. The works embrace the range of styles encountered in American art, including realism, romanticism, impressionism, and expressionism.

The subject of the American West—its land, people, and wildlife—is the linking thread. In the Whitney Gallery, the West can be seen as a specific place embodied in scenes of the Rocky Mountains, Indian encampments, cattle ranches, and other physical places in the region. The West is also an idea, or even a myth, interpreted in the visions of an American Eden, an untamed wilderness, and a land of opportunity, courage,

and cultural values.

In chronological terms, the Whitney collection includes paintings by such early explorer artists as George Catlin, Alfred Jacob Miller, and John Mix Stanley. The glories of the western lands are revealed in landscapes by Albert Bierstadt and Thomas Moran. Frederic Remington and Charles M. Russell lead the artists who depicted the wild West at the turn of the century and influenced early twentieth-century illustrators such as N. C. Wyeth and W. H. D. Koerner. Finally, the Whitney Gallery exhibits paintings and sculptures by contemporary artists, such as James Bama, Fritz Scholder, and Harry Jackson, whose works represent viewpoints on the modern West.

Such paintings, sculptures, and prints have helped to shape our concepts of the meaning of the West. These masterworks celebrate the artistic impulse enriched by the American encounter with the West.

ABOVE:
FREDERIC REMINGTON (1861–1909).
RADISSON AND GROSEILLIERS, 1905.
OIL ON CANVAS; 17⅛ x 30⅛ IN.
Remington became one of the most famous western artists through his archetypal depictions of the wild West—bucking broncos, danger, and conflict. Late in his career, as he loosened his brushstrokes and experimented with color, he painted masterworks such as *Radisson and Groseilliers* which portray a more harmonious encounter with the frontier.
Gift of Mrs. Karl Frank.

BELOW/RIGHT (DETAIL):
PAUL MANSHIP (1885–1966).
INDIAN AND PRONGHORN ANTELOPE, 1914.
BRONZE; INDIAN, HEIGHT 13½ IN.; ANTELOPE, HEIGHT 12½ IN.
Manship united a classical concern for precisely modeled forms with a modern streamlined sensibility, creating a style that was a forerunner of Art Deco. Interested in mythology, he portrayed the American Indian not with anthropological realism, but as a symbolic figure evoking the power of the hunt.
Gift of the William E. Weiss Fund and Mr. and Mrs. Richard J. Schwartz.

WILLIAM TYLEE RANNEY (1813–1857).
ADVICE ON THE PRAIRIE, 1853.
OIL ON CANVAS; 38¾ x 55¼ IN.
Ranney painted genre paintings, scenes of everyday life on the American frontier. In this work he portrayed a group of western immigrants, including a family, camped with their wagon for the evening. A mountain man, the representative of an earlier period of frontier history, tells them tales of what they will encounter.
Gift of Mrs. J. Maxwell Moran.

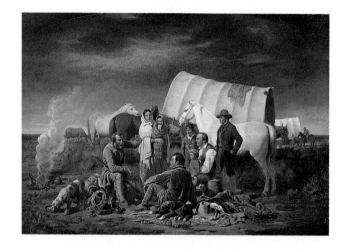

GEORGE CATLIN (1796–1872).
RAIN-MAKING, MANDAN, C. 1855–1870.
OIL ON CARDBOARD ON BRISTOL;
18⅛ x 24⅝ IN.
Believing that Indians soon would vanish, Catlin traveled west with the mission of recording tribal customs and appearances to preserve them. He saw the Indian as a primitive man, living in unity with nature. Self-taught, Catlin developed a simplified style with strong lines and bold contrasts of color.
Gift of Paul Mellon.

RIGHT:
ALBERT BIERSTADT (1820–1902).
YELLOWSTONE FALLS, C. 1881.
OIL ON CANVAS; 44¼ x 30½ IN.
Bierstadt painted this view of the Lower Falls after his 1881 trip to Yellowstone National Park. He loaned this painting to the White House and tried to convince Congress to purchase it for the President's residence, but was never successful. It helped, however, to inspire President Chester A. Arthur to visit Yellowstone in 1883.
Gift of Mr. and Mrs. Lloyd Taggart.

JOHN MIX STANLEY (1814–1872).
LAST OF THEIR RACE, 1857.
OIL ON CANVAS; 43 x 60 IN.
An allegory on the theme of the Indian as a dying race, this painting depicts remnants of the tribes pushed to the edge of the ocean with the sun setting in the distance and buffalo skulls forecasting the end. Stanley arranged his representatives of the tribes and ages in a pyramid, giving a classical composition to the painting.

ROSA BONHEUR (1822–1899).
COL. WILLIAM F. CODY, 1889.
OIL ON CANVAS; 18½ x 15¼ IN.
Buffalo Bill enthralled Europeans
with his Wild West exhibition when
he took it to Paris in 1889. He
accepted the invitation of Rosa
Bonheur to visit her chateau in
Fontainebleau, where she probably
painted this portrait. She in turn
visited the grounds of Cody's Wild
West to sketch the exotic American
animals.
*Given in Memory of William R. Coe
and Mai Rogers Coe.*

THOMAS MORAN (1837–1926).
*THE GOLDEN GATE,
YELLOWSTONE NATIONAL PARK*, 1893.
OIL ON CANVAS; 36¼ x 50¼ IN.
Moran's name became synonymous
with Yellowstone. After he accompanied the official governmental
expedition into the region in 1871,
his sketches of the wonders helped
to convince Congress to establish
Yellowstone as the first national
park. The artist returned to the
Park in 1892 and painted this view
of the Golden Gate pass.

TOP RIGHT:
HENRY FARNY (1847–1916).
DAYS OF LONG AGO, 1903.
OIL ON PAPER MOUNTED ON BOARD;
37½ x 23¾ IN.

Farny traveled west as a magazine illustrator at the end of the nineteenth century and was familiar with changes affecting Native American life after the Indian wars. In easel paintings such as *Days of Long Ago* he created nostalgic visions of a bygone past.

N. C. WYETH (1882–1945).
THE LEE OF THE GRUB-WAGON,
1904–1905.
OIL ON CANVAS; 38 x 26 IN.

In 1904 Wyeth made his first trip to the West. He worked for three weeks on a Colorado cattle roundup, which provided the inspiration for a series of paintings about cowboys.
Gift of John M. Schiff.

CHARLES M. RUSSELL (1864–1926).
WHEN LAW DULLS THE EDGE OF CHANCE, 1915.
OIL ON CANVAS; 30x48 IN.

Known as the "cowboy artist," Russell is often appreciated for his insider's view of western life. His own experiences as a wrangler informed his paintings and sculpture, but he also used historical events and imagination in works such as this depiction of horse thieves intercepted by the Royal Canadian Mounted Police.

Gift of William E. Weiss.

MAYNARD DIXON (1875–1946).
THE MEDICINE ROBE, 1915.
OIL ON CANVAS; 40x30 IN.

Experimenting with an impressionistic painting style and drawing upon his experiences working in the desert light of the West, California-born Dixon created this powerful image of a Northern Plains Indian.

Gift of Mr. and Mrs. Godwin Pelissero.

JOSEPH HENRY SHARP (1859–1953).
THE BROKEN BOW, C. 1912.
OIL ON CANVAS; 44½ x 59⅜ IN.
In the early years of the twentieth century, Sharp divided his time between painting the Northern Plains Indians of Montana and the Southwestern Indians of New Mexico. In this tender subject of family life, he combined the two groups, using Plains clothing and an adobe setting.

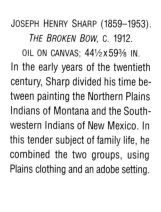

FREDERIC REMINGTON (1861–1909).
THE RATTLESNAKE, C. 1905; REWORKED 1908; CAST C. 1909.
BRONZE; CAST NO. 17, ROMAN BRONZE WORKS;
HEIGHT 22⅝ IN.
Remington used the subject of the horse reacting to the rattlesnake to create one of his most daring sculptures. He modeled the horse as a dynamic curve pulling away from the small, but deadly snake. Dissatisfied with his first version of this sculpture, Remington reworked it extensively to create this larger, more compact version.
Gift of The Coe Foundation.

W. H. D. KOERNER (1878–1938).
MADONNA OF THE PRAIRIE, 1921.
OIL ON CANVAS; 37 x 28¾ IN.
In the novel *The Covered Wagon*,
Molly Wingate traveled the Oregon
Trail with a wagon train of settlers.
Encountering prairie fires and Indian
arrows, the beautiful maiden even-
tually reached Oregon, where, in
the conventions of popular fiction,
she found true love. In this illus-
tration for the book jacket of the
novel, Koerner used the covered
wagon to form a halo around the
pioneer's head.

JAMES EARLE FRASER (1876–1953).
THE END OF THE TRAIL,
MODELED 1894; REWORKED 1915; CAST AFTER 1918.
BRONZE; CAST BY ROMAN BRONZE WORKS; HEIGHT 33¾ IN.
The End of the Trail has appealed to public sentiment since
its conception following Chicago's 1893 World's Columbian
Exposition. Inspired by the exposition's fusing of the
nostalgic with the progressive, Fraser created a windblown
and destitute symbol which represented the public's
belief in the sad but inevitable extinction of the Indian.
Clara Peck Purchase Fund.

JAMES BAMA (B. 1926).
A CONTEMPORARY SIOUX INDIAN, 1978.
OIL ON PANEL; 23⅜ x 35⅜ IN.

A Contemporary Sioux Indian is Bama's statement on the rejection of traditional Native American culture in mainstream American society. The decaying background reads NO PARKING VIOLATORS TOWED AWAY. The artist's realistic style comes from an attentive painting method which uses both photographs and sketches as preparation.
William E. Weiss Contemporary Art Fund.

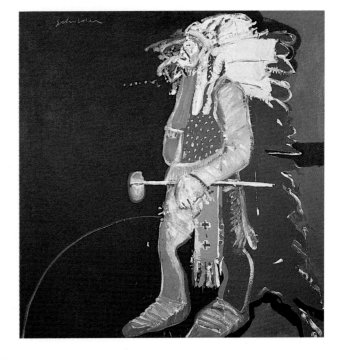

FRITZ SCHOLDER (B. 1937).
INDIAN WITH TOMAHAWK, 1970.
OIL ON CANVAS; 58¼ x 58¼ IN.

In a series on Indians begun in 1967, Scholder sought new and innovative pictorial representations to convey the harsh realities of the contemporary Indian's world. He often uses bold, unnatural colors and distorted images with loose painterly brush work to create his personal vision of the Indian's reality.
William E. Weiss Contemporary Art Fund.

The experiences of the Plains Indian people include some of the most dramatic episodes in the history of the American West. The people known by the tribal names of Arapaho, Cheyenne, Kiowa, Comanche, Blackfeet, Sioux, Shoshone, and Pawnee, among others, once dominated the vast open region of the Great Plains stretching from the Mississippi River to the Rocky Mountains. Through its outstanding collections and interpretive programs, the Plains Indian Museum explores the cultural histories and artistry of these people from their buffalo hunting past to the living traditions of the present.

At the beginning of the nineteenth century, the people of the Plains lived as farmers in villages along streams and fertile river valleys, and as hunters in tipi camps in the tall grass prairies where vast herds of buffalo grazed. Their food and most important necessities were taken from the buffalo, deer, elk, and other game, and wild plant resources of the region. From the warriors' feathered war bonnets, shields, and lances to their hide clothing, moccasins, and ceremonial rattles and fans, objects were beautifully decorated with natural pigments, porcupine quills, and trade beads.

By the end of the nineteenth century Plains Indian people faced confinement on reservations, which ended their lives as buffalo hunters. The clothing and ceremonial objects of reservation life illustrate not only older traditions, but also the introduction of new ideas, materials, and designs.

The Contemporary Gallery of the Plains Indian Museum completes the story of the survival of the Plains people and their most important traditions. The beadwork, powwow clothing, paintings, sculptures, and other examples of contemporary art reflect this cultural survival in a changing world.

TOP:
EAGLE HAT, CROW, C. 1870.
LENGTH 26 IN.; HEIGHT 11 IN.
With its special power and beauty, the eagle is the bird most revered by Plains Indian people. This hat is composed of an eagle head, wing, and tail feathers over buffalo hide; it is trimmed with brass bells and has brass button eyes.
*Gift of
Mr. and Mrs. I. H. "Larry" Larom.*

RIGHT:
GRIZZLY BEAR CLAW NECKLACE,
MADE BY JOHN YOUNG BEAR,
MESQUAKIE, C. 1920.
CIRCLE: LENGTH 12 IN.; WIDTH 6½ IN.
TRAILER: LENGTH 60 IN.
Worn by men of the Eastern Plains, grizzly bear claw necklaces were highly valued, because they reflected the strength and courage of the bear. This necklace is made of otter fur, beads, and forty bear claws.
*Adolph Spohr Collection,
Gift of Larry Sheerin.*

ABOVE:
DRESS, SIOUX, C. 1900. LENGTH 45 IN.
Since the late 1800s, Sioux women have created dresses with heavily beaded yokes in bold designs. This type of dress was worn only for special occasions.
Gift of Mr. and Mrs. William Henry Harrison.

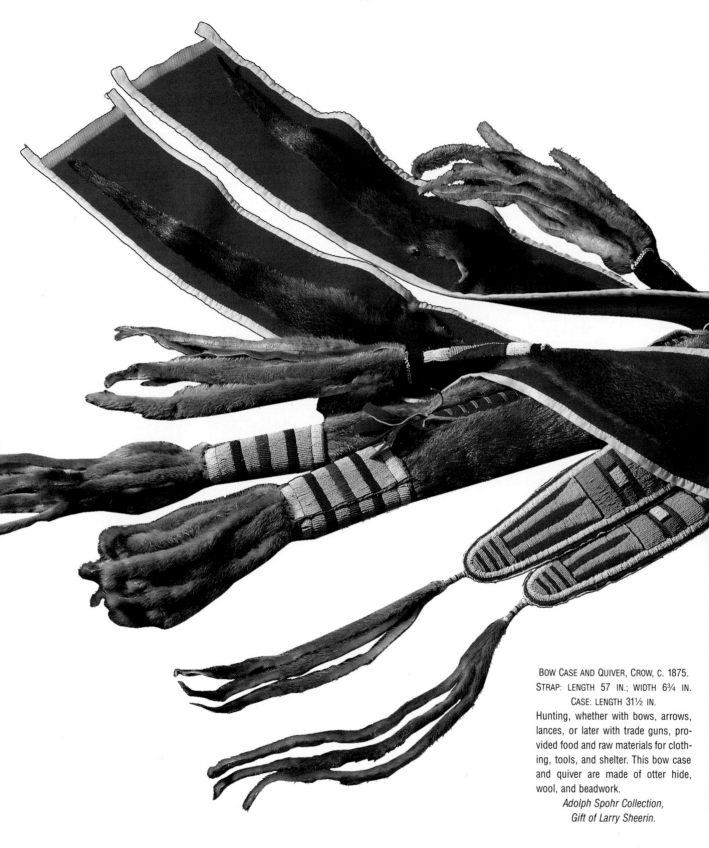

BOW CASE AND QUIVER, CROW, C. 1875.
STRAP: LENGTH 57 IN.; WIDTH 6¾ IN.
CASE: LENGTH 31½ IN.
Hunting, whether with bows, arrows, lances, or later with trade guns, provided food and raw materials for clothing, tools, and shelter. This bow case and quiver are made of otter hide, wool, and beadwork.
Adolph Spohr Collection,
Gift of Larry Sheerin.

Shields were made of thick pieces of rawhide and painted with symbols created to provide strength to the warrior. Animal figures were frequently used designs on both shields and their covers.

SHIELD COVER, CROW, C. 1870.
DIAMETER 19¼ IN.
This shield cover is made of buckskin, buffalo hide, and ermine.
*Adolph Spohr Collection,
Gift of Larry Sheerin.*

SHIELD COVER, CROW, C. 1860.
DIAMETER 21½ IN.
A painted bear and his tracks, a charm, and a flicker feather make up the design of this buckskin shield cover.
Chandler-Pohrt Collection, Gift of Mr. and Mrs. Edson W. Spencer.

RIGHT:
PARFLECHE, CHEYENNE, C. 1885.
LENGTH 23½ IN.; WIDTH 14¾ IN.
Parfleches made of folded rawhide were used to carry clothing, food, and other belongings when Plains Indian people traveled. Painted in geometric designs, parfleches often were made in pairs to be tied to each side of the horse.
Chandler-Pohrt Collection.

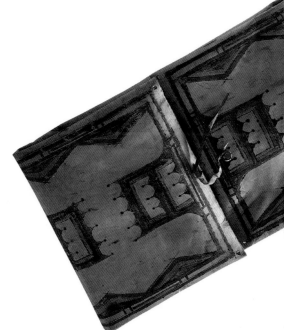

SADDLE BLANKET,
NORTHERN PLAINS, C. 1835.
LENGTH 61 IN.; WIDTH 27¾ IN.
This saddle blanket from the Northern Plains is made of hide, tradecloth, pony beads, and tin cones.
Chandler-Pohrt Collection.

MAN'S LEGGINGS,
UPPER MISSOURI, C. 1835.
LENGTH 50 IN.; WIDTH 12½ IN.
Clothing for the Plains warrior and buffalo hunter was functional yet reflected a sense of design. Leggings such as these were painted or decorated with beads acquired from traders.
Chandler-Pohrt Collection.

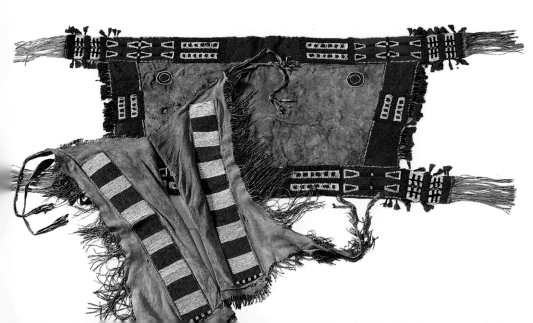

In 1890 Plains Indian people faced poverty, disease, and death on reservations. Under the leadership of the Paiute visionary, Wovoka, the Ghost Dance religion revived the hopes of many of the tribes. Wovoka taught that the people could bring about the renewal of the world by working hard, living peacefully, and doing the Ghost Dance. The buffalo and other game would be plentiful, dead relatives and friends would return, and white men would disappear.

GHOST DANCE DRESS,
ARAPAHO, C. 1890.
LENGTH 54 IN.
The Arapaho were instrumental in spreading the doctrines of the Ghost Dance to other tribes. The design of this Arapaho dress depicts the crescent moon and the stars, represented by crosses.
Chandler-Pohrt Collection.

GHOST DANCE DRESS,
SOUTHERN PLAINS, C. 1890.
LENGTH 56 IN.
Hide dresses, shirts, and leggings
with painted symbols of the sky
such as the stars and moon were
made for the Ghost Dance.
Gift of J. C. Kid Nichols.

GHOST DANCE SHIRT,
ARAPAHO, C. 1890.
LENGTH 40 IN.
Designs for Ghost Dance clothing
often came to individuals in visions
that occurred during the ceremonies. The turtle, seen on this
shirt, was symbolic to the Arapaho
of the spirit world. Eagles, crows,
and magpies were considered mes-
sengers to the heavens.
*Chandler-Pohrt Collection,
Gift of The Searle Family Trust
and The Paul Stock Foundation.*

SALISH CRADLE, 1919.
LENGTH 34½ IN.; WIDTH 15 IN.
Cradles continued to be made and
used after Plains Indian people left
the buffalo hunting way of life. This
beaded Salish cradle with floral designs could have been made for a
special occasion.
Gift of J. R. Simplot.

OSAGE CRADLE, C. 1900.
LENGTH 42 IN.;
WIDTH 11¼ IN.; DEPTH 12 IN.
The making of a cradle was undertaken by the family of a newborn baby with prayers and care to assure the child would have a long, healthy life. Tribal designs, such as the carved and painted wood pattern and fingerwoven sash of this Osage cradle, were distinctive.
Chandler-Pohrt Collection.

CROW CRADLE, C. 1900.
LENGTH 40¾ IN.; WIDTH 10¾ IN.
Among Plains Indian people, both men and women had important economic roles. A beautifully decorated cradle such as this Crow example provided a safe place for the baby while women worked and when the family traveled by horseback.
Katherine Bradford McClellan Collection,
Gift of The Coe Foundation.

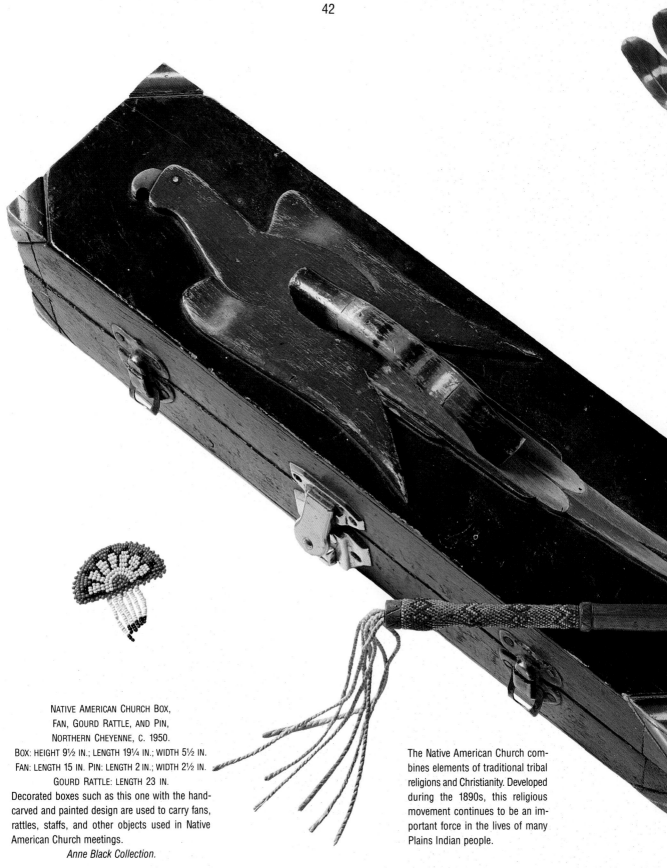

NATIVE AMERICAN CHURCH BOX,
FAN, GOURD RATTLE, AND PIN,
NORTHERN CHEYENNE, C. 1950.
BOX: HEIGHT 9½ IN.; LENGTH 19¼ IN.; WIDTH 5½ IN.
FAN: LENGTH 15 IN. PIN: LENGTH 2 IN.; WIDTH 2½ IN.
GOURD RATTLE: LENGTH 23 IN.
Decorated boxes such as this one with the hand-
carved and painted design are used to carry fans,
rattles, staffs, and other objects used in Native
American Church meetings.
Anne Black Collection.

The Native American Church com-
bines elements of traditional tribal
religions and Christianity. Developed
during the 1890s, this religious
movement continues to be an important force in the lives of many
Plains Indian people.

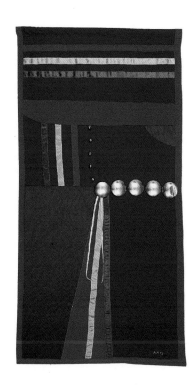

BANNER, MADE BY ARTHUR AMIOTTE,
SIOUX, 1972.
LENGTH 52 IN.; WIDTH 27 IN.
This banner blends old traditions
within a new form. Made of wool,
satin, bells, and ribbons, this banner represents a typical ribbon
dress with a silver belt of the late
eighteenth and early nineteenth
centuries.

CROSS, MADE BY MITCHELL ZEPHER,
SIOUX, C. 1979.
LENGTH 9 IN.; WIDTH 4½ IN.
This nickel silver and brass cross
is made up of designs associated
with the Native American Church.
On the cross can be seen the crescent and waterbird, and the gourd
rattle, staff, and water drum used
in the ceremonies.

The Cody Firearms Museum is the largest and most important collection of American firearms in the world. Its nearly five thousand objects chronicle the development of firearms from the sixteenth century to the present. Replicas of a colonial gun shop, a late nineteenth-century factory, a frontier stage stop, and a western hardware store document the influence of firearms on the settlement of the United States and the fundamental contributions of the firearms industry to the industrial revolution.

At the heart of the Cody Firearms Museum is the Winchester Arms Collection. Previously housed at the Winchester factory in New Haven, Connecticut, the collection came to the Buffalo Bill Historical Center in 1975, on long-term loan from the Olin Corporation. Prior to the construction of the Cody Firearms Museum, the Winchester Collection was displayed from 1976 to 1981 in conjunction with the Buffalo Bill Museum. Beginning in 1981 it was displayed separately as the Winchester Arms Museum, in a specially designed gallery on the lower level. The collection was formally given to the Center by the Olin Corporation in 1988. Construction of the new wing was completed in the spring of 1991, and the Cody Firearms Museum opened to the public on June 22, 1991.

In addition to its encyclopedic firearms collection, which represents the work of most major American arms makers, the Cody Firearms Museum has an important research collection of thousands of nineteenth and early twentieth-century engineering and design drawings, production records, and advertising materials. The collection also includes the personal records of Rudolf J. Kornbrath, one of America's foremost firearms engravers of the early twentieth century.

TOP:
GERMAN FLINTLOCK POCKET PISTOL,
C. 1710. .33 CALIBER.
OVERALL LENGTH 5⅞ IN.;
BARREL LENGTH 2¾ IN.
Even before the introduction of the well-known Deringer pistol of the nineteenth century, small pistols such as this one made by Weber of Berlin were popular personal sidearms.

RIGHT:
WINCHESTER MODEL 1895
SPORTING RIFLE,
SERIAL NUMBER 403148,
C. 1924. .30-06 CALIBER.
OVERALL LENGTH 42 IN.;
BARREL LENGTH 24 IN.; HEIGHT 7¾ IN.
This highly decorated sporting rifle was presented to novelist Zane Gray by the Winchester Repeating Arms Company.
Gift of Mrs. Margaret T. Moore Kane.

ABOVE:
ENGINEERING DESIGN DRAWINGS AND WINCHESTER SAMPLE MODEL 1893 SHOTGUN.
Design drawings are critical elements in the development of firearms. These drawings help to document the design processes which accompanied the creation of the Model 1893 shotgun as well as other models.

ABOVE:
ENGLISH BREECH-LOADING FLINTLOCK PISTOL,
C. 1720. .62 CALIBER.
OVERALL LENGTH 11¾ IN.; BARREL LENGTH 5⅛ IN.
Turn-off pistols were among the most popular breech-loading firearms of the seventeenth and eighteenth centuries. Made by H. Delaney of London, the pistol is loaded by unscrewing the barrel and placing a charge directly into the breech

RIGHT:
SOUTH GERMAN WHEEL LOCK CARBINE,
DATED 1596. .40 CALIBER.
OVERALL LENGTH 35½ IN.; BARREL LENGTH 24½ IN.
Made for Grand Duke Christian II, Elector of Saxony, this wheel lock carbine provides an excellent example of the exquisite decoration that graced luxury arms of the sixteenth century.

AMERICAN AND EUROPEAN POWDER HORNS AND FLASKS,
MID-NINETEENTH CENTURY.
This group of powder horns and flasks is representative
of those commonly used in North America and Europe
between 1780 and 1850.

48

EUROPEAN FLINTLOCK MUSKETS,
FOWLERS, AND FUSILS,
MID-EIGHTEENTH TO
MID-NINETEENTH CENTURIES.
During the Colonial period, America
relied on Europe for her firearms.
Most muskets used by American
forces during the Revolution were
imported. Even hunting guns, such
as fowlers, assembled in America,
were usually fitted with foreign-
made barrels and flintlocks. The
well-made European flintlock fusil
was the Native Americans' choice
of firearm well into the nineteenth
century.

ENGLISH FLINTLOCK PISTOL,
C. 1800. .50 CALIBER.
OVERALL LENGTH 8¾ IN.; BARREL LENGTH 2½ IN.
Commonly known as a "Duck's Foot" pistol,
this example made by Goodwin & Company
of London was designed for use by British
naval officers. Its four barrels fired simul-
taneously, a distinct advantage if its user
were attacked.

AMERICAN PERCUSSION RIFLE,
C. 1815. .43 CALIBER.
OVERALL LENGTH 52¼ IN.; BARREL LENGTH 36 IN.
Soon after its development in England, the percus-
sion ignition system spread to the United States.
This Pennsylvania-style rifle made by Coe was fitted
with a pill-lock percussion ignition system rather
than the traditional flintlock.

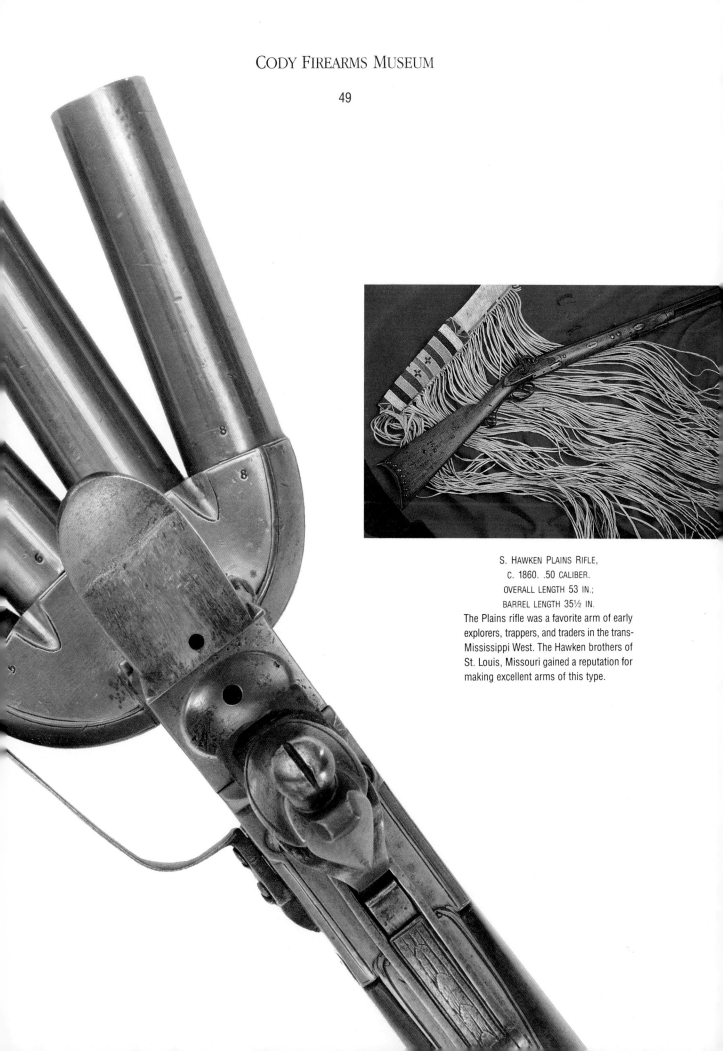

S. HAWKEN PLAINS RIFLE,
C. 1860. .50 CALIBER.
OVERALL LENGTH 53 IN.;
BARREL LENGTH 35½ IN.

The Plains rifle was a favorite arm of early explorers, trappers, and traders in the trans-Mississippi West. The Hawken brothers of St. Louis, Missouri gained a reputation for making excellent arms of this type.

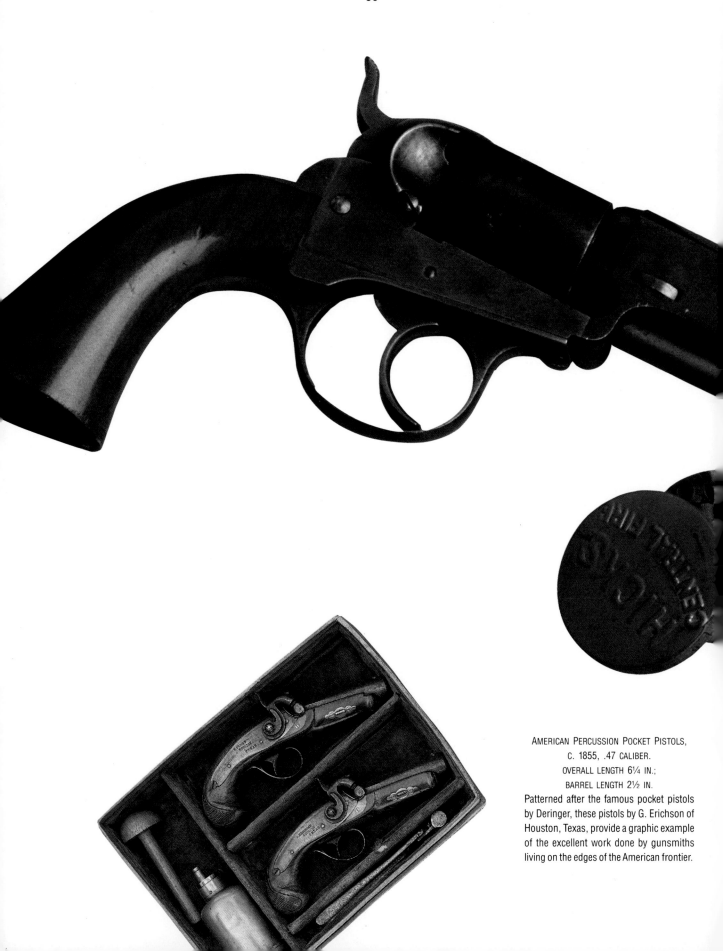

AMERICAN PERCUSSION POCKET PISTOLS,
C. 1855, .47 CALIBER.
OVERALL LENGTH 6¼ IN.;
BARREL LENGTH 2½ IN.

Patterned after the famous pocket pistols by Deringer, these pistols by G. Erichson of Houston, Texas, provide a graphic example of the excellent work done by gunsmiths living on the edges of the American frontier.

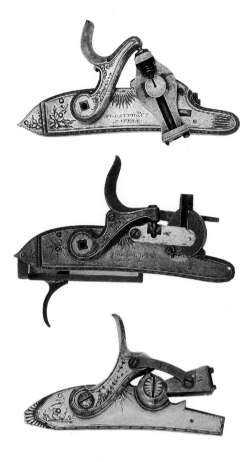

ENGLISH AND FRENCH
DETACHED PERCUSSION PISTOL LOCKS,
C. 1805–1820.
The Rev. Alexander Forsyth, a Scottish minister, was an avid sportsman and inventor. His invention of the percussion ignition system was the most important development in the evolution of firearms since the introduction of gunpowder.

COLT MODEL 1873 SINGLE ACTION REVOLVER,
SERIAL NUMBER 51193, C. 1880.
.44 CALIBER. BARREL LENGTH 7½ IN.
Also known as the "Peacemaker" and "Frontier Six-shooter," the Colt Model 1873 is the revolver that most think of as a symbol of the wild West.
Gift of Mrs. Lillian E. Herring.

COLT MODEL 1855 PERCUSSION
POCKET PISTOL, SERIAL NUMBER 17,
MADE IN 1855. .28 CALIBER.
OVERALL LENGTH 7¾ IN.;
BARREL LENGTH 3¼ IN.
Over the years the name Colt has become a synonym for the revolver. This Model 1855 pocket pistol was engraved by Gustave Young, one of the foremost American engravers of the nineteenth century.
Gift of Larry Sheerin.

FIREARMS FACTORY REPLICA.
During the late nineteenth century the firearms industry was responsible for many of the design innovations that made modern manufacturing methods possible. Many of the machines in use today have their origins in the firearms factories of that period.

WINCHESTER MODEL 1894 LEVER ACTION RIFLE,
SERIAL NUMBER 154222,
MADE IN 1902. .30 CALIBER.
OVERALL LENGTH 44½ IN.; BARREL LENGTH 26 IN.
Several members of the renowned Ulrich family of engravers worked for the Winchester Repeating Arms Company. This deluxe takedown version of the Model 1894 was engraved and inlaid with gold by John Ulrich.

J.M. COOPER PERCUSSION POCKET REVOLVER, SERIAL NUMBER 403, C. 1864. .31 CALIBER. OVERALL LENGTH 11 IN.; BARREL LENGTH 6 IN. Manufactured in Pittsburgh, Pennsylvania, Cooper pocket revolvers bore a strong resemblance to the Colt Model 1849. About 15,000 pocket and Navy model pistols were made by the Cooper Company between 1862 and 1869.

CYLINDERS FOR AMERICAN AND EUROPEAN REVOLVERS, NINETEENTH AND TWENTIETH CENTURIES. Although firearms equipped with revolving cylinders had been made for some time, they were not produced in large numbers until the middle of the nineteenth century.

MCCRACKEN RESEARCH LIBRARY

Named for Dr. Harold McCracken, founding director of the Buffalo Bill Historical Center, the McCracken Research Library was dedicated and opened to the public on August 15, 1980. Dr. McCracken's lifelong search for knowledge and his dedication to research and scholarship are guiding principles for the Library. With collections in western American art and history, Plains Indian ethnography and art, and firearms history and technology, the Library provides a solid foundation of both contemporary and retrospective works for research.

Besides books, the Library has several important manuscript collections directly related to the artifacts in the Center's museums. One of the largest and most used collections is the William F. Cody Archives, which include personal correspondence, Wild West programs and route books, scrapbooks, pulp novels, sheet music, poetry, photographs, and ephemera. In conjunction with the Buffalo Bill Museum collection, the archives provide an overview of Cody's life and career, as well as insight into Cody as an individual and showman.

Three of the manuscript collections document the lives and works of artists Joseph H. Sharp, W. H. D. Koerner, and Frank Tenney Johnson. The Koerner Archives supplement the Koerner Studio Collection in the Whitney Gallery of Western Art, while the Frank Tenney Johnson material presents one of the most comprehensive primary source collections in existence. In addition, the Library also has manuscript and photograph collections documenting the nineteenth and twentieth century American cowboy and Plains Indian, the dude ranch industry, and the prehistoric cultures of northern Wyoming. The Library's holdings are available to staff, visiting scholars, museum patrons, and visitors. Library materials are also on exhibit in each of the museums.

ABOVE:
STEREOSCOPE, C. 1904.
LENGTH 12 IN.;
HEIGHT 3 IN.; WIDTH 7 IN.
Wood and tin stereoscope shown holding one of nearly two hundred stereoscopic views in the Yellowstone National Park Collection. The McCracken Library collections of photographs, woodcuts and engravings, books, pamphlets, maps, and ephemera portray the human history of "Wonderland," the nation's first national park.

RIGHT:
WILLIAM CULLEN BRYANT.
PICTURESQUE AMERICA.
NEW YORK: APPLETON AND CO., 1872.
From important works illuminating the "newly" discovered continent, to the novels of the early twentieth century, illustrated books provide an important resource for studying and understanding how Americans viewed the West.

The spirit of the American West has long been captured in song. From cowboy songs and range ballads to songs from Buffalo Bill's Wild West, the McCracken Library preserves the musical heritage of the West in both written and recorded form.

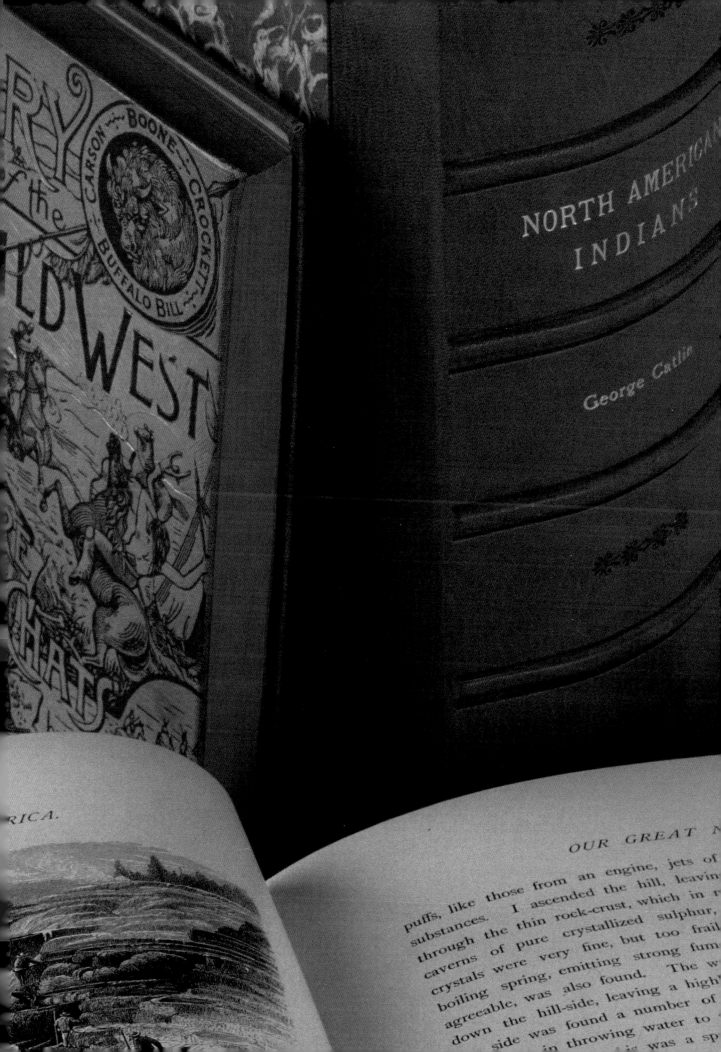

A selection of material in the Yellowstone National Park Special Collection that advertised the wonders of the region. Through illustrations, photographs, and pamphlets such as these, railroads, tour companies, and other commercial ventures hoped to lure visitors to the park.

Grace Raymond Hebard and Paul M. Paine.
Map of the History and Romance of Wyoming,
reprint, 1936.
One of the many maps in the Library collections that trace the exploration and settlement of Wyoming from pre-territorial days to the present.

GEORGE A. CUSTER.
MY LIFE ON THE PLAINS.
NEW YORK: SHELDON AND CO., 1874.
The Indian wars period, 1865–1890,
was one of conflict and change in
the American West. Books, maps,
and photographs from and about
this period form an important core
collection in the Research Library.

BOARD OF TRUSTEES

COPYRIGHT ©1992
BY BUFFALO BILL HISTORICAL CENTER.
All Rights Reserved. No portion of this
book may be reproduced, copied, or dup-
licated by any means, or by any system
including data storage or tape recording
without prior written consent. Reviewers
exempted from above restrictions for
the purpose of quoting brief passages
in connection with a review, or inclusion
in a newspaper, magazine, or journal.
ISBN 0931618371
PRODUCED FOR
THE BUFFALO BILL HISTORICAL CENTER
BY LEGACY PUBLISHING,
2020 Alameda Padre Serra,
Santa Barbara, CA 93103.
Printed and bound in Hong Kong
by Golden Cup Printing.
PHOTOGRAPHY BY
Devendra Shrikhande
Buffalo Bill Historical Center
DESIGN BY
Matt Hahn
PROJECT COORDINATION BY
Courtney Fischer and Matt Hahn